Meet my Neighbor

Meet my neighbor, the chef

Marc Crabtree

Author and Photographer

🌳 Crabtree Publishing Company

www.crabtreebooks.com

Crabtree Publishing Company

Meet my neighbor, the chef

For Neil and Nancy, with thanks

Author and photographer
Marc Crabtree

Editor
Reagan Miller

Design
Samantha Crabtree

Production coordinator
Margaret Amy Salter

Glossary
Crystal Sikkens

Photographs
All photographs by Marc Crabtree except:
iStock: page 3

Library and Archives Canada Cataloguing in Publication

Crabtree, Marc
    Meet my neighbor, the chef / author and photographer, Marc Crabtree.

(Meet my neighbor)
ISBN 978-0-7787-4571-6 (bound).--ISBN 978-0-7787-4581-5 (pbk.)

    1. Noseworthy, Neil--Juvenile literature. 2. Cookery--Juvenile literature.
3. Cooks--Canada--Biography--Juvenile literature. I. Crabtree, Marc. Meet
my neighbor. II. Title. III. Series.

TX714.C73 2009   j641.5092   C2009-900422-4

Library of Congress Cataloging-in-Publication Data

Crabtree, Marc.
  Meet my neighbor, the chef / author and photographer, Marc
Crabtree.
       p. cm. -- (Meet my neighbor)
  ISBN 978-0-7787-4581-5 (pbk. : alk. paper) -- ISBN 978-0-7787-4571-6
(reinforced library binding : alk. paper)
  1. Cookery--Juvenile literature. 2. Cooks--Juvenile literature. I. Title.
II. Series.

TX714.C7223 2009
641.5092--dc22
                                                    2009001650

Crabtree Publishing Company

Printed in Canada/092018/MQ20180817

www.crabtreebooks.com   1-800-387-7650

Published in Canada
Crabtree Publishing
616 Welland Ave.
St. Catharines, Ontario
L2M 5V6

Published in the United States
Crabtree Publishing
PMB 59051
350 Fifth Avenue, 59th Floor
New York, New York 10118

Published in the United Kingdom
Crabtree Publishing
Maritime House
Basin Road North, Hove
BN41 1WR

Published in Australia
Crabtree Publishing
3 Charles Street
Coburg North
VIC, 3058

Meet my Neighbor

Contents

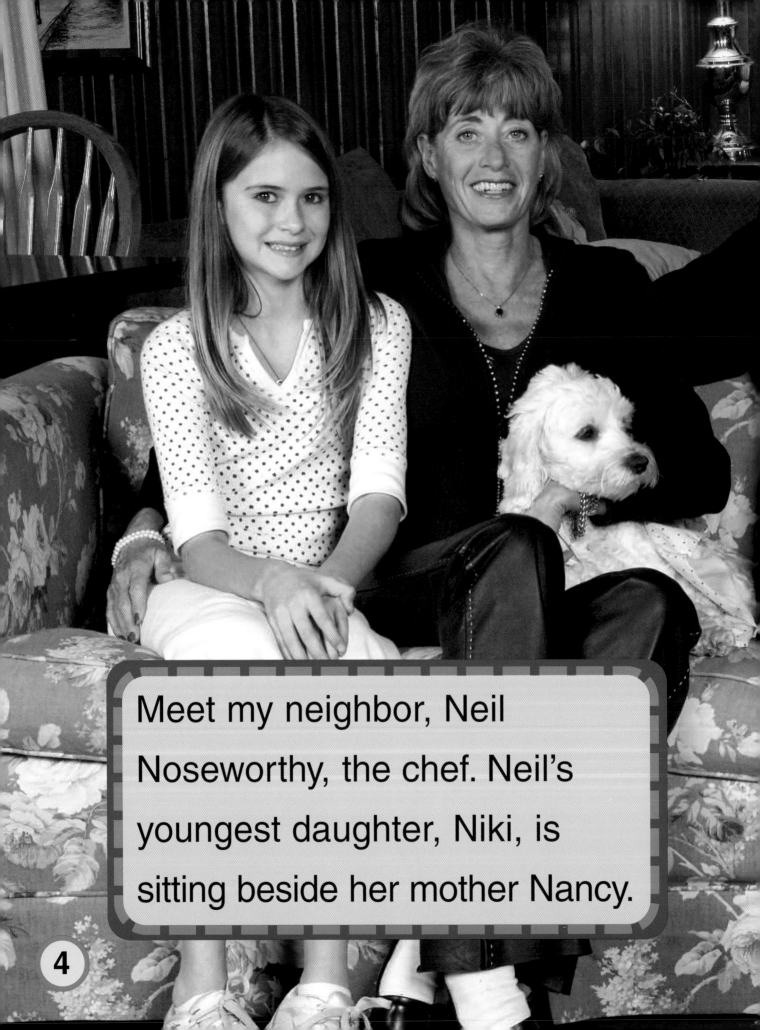

Meet my neighbor, Neil Noseworthy, the chef. Neil's youngest daughter, Niki, is sitting beside her mother Nancy.

Nancy's dog is a cockapoo called Princess. Neil's oldest daughter Natalie is sitting with her dog, Shadow.

Niki has invited her friend Zena for supper. Natalie is hidden behind her mother. The girls helped their father cook **tacos** for dinner.

Neil is going to prepare the food for a wedding party. He checks the list of foods he has to buy.

Neil squeezes an **avocado** to make sure it is fresh.

Neil has a large walk-in **refrigerator**.
It keeps the food for the party cold.

11

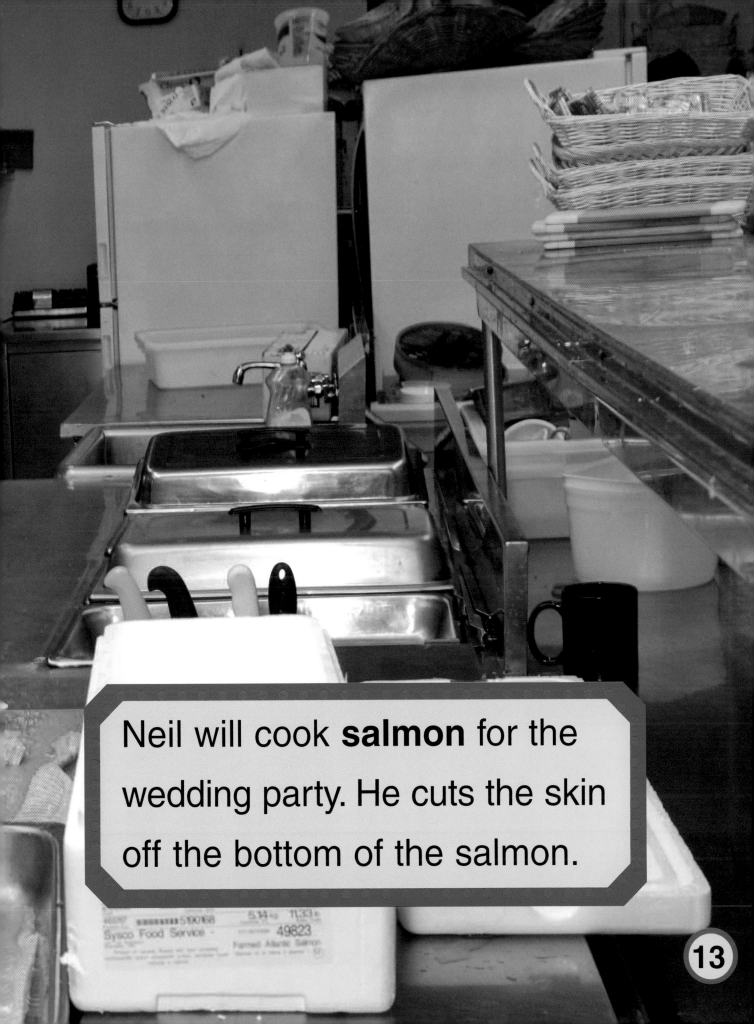

Neil will cook **salmon** for the wedding party. He cuts the skin off the bottom of the salmon.

Neil and his helpers put the cooked food on plates. The plates will be served to the people at the party.

Neil's servers carry the meals out to the wedding guests.

A server brings the **bride** her meal. The bride and **groom** are sitting in front of the guests.

Neil and his helper put the **cheesecake** on plates.

Neil pours caramel over the cheesecake. It will be served for dessert.

The groom thanks Neil for the wonderful meal.

On the right is the mother of the bride. Thanks to Neil's meal, everyone is happy and full.

Glossary

avocado

bride

cheesecake

groom

refrigerator

salmon

tacos